ABOUT THE AUTHOR

Leah Atherton is a linguist, poet and runner based in Birmingham, UK. She had poems about her adventures featured by iRunFar and Porridge magazines and Brum Radio Poets. Elsewhere, her work has appeared in Birmingham Art Gallery and on BBC Radio WM, and was included as part of the Beatfreeks Collective anniversary anthology, *Wild Dreams and Louder Voices* (Verve Poetry Press, 2018)

She believes in strong coffee, campfire whisky and the power of muddy shoes.

You can find her on Instagram @poet_on_the_run

Leah Atherton

A sky the colour of hope

VERVE
POETRY PRESS

BIRMINGHAM

PUBLISHED BY VERVE POETRY PRESS
https://vervepoetrypress.com
mail@vervepoetrypress.com

FIRST PUBLISHED JULY 2020

Printed and bound in the UK
by ImprintDigital, Exeter

ISBN: 978-1-912565-39-9

Cover photo credit: wildseascapes.co.uk

For Papa –

I think I understand now.

CONTENTS

A sky the colour of hope

Storage unit

When I crack the lock,
you see that there is nowhere
near enough dust.

Everything here is visited often,
handled with care;
lifted to the sunlight
and brushed off.

This is where I keep the poems.

Trail magic

They say that salt water is a great purifier
So I will run to the sea
Turn my bones to salt in the river of my steps
Ask to return to something bigger than I am.

Let me arrive undone from pretences,
Shedding my layers of regret, of doubt;
Let me arrive naked as will and saltwater skin
Because what is prayer, really,
If not stripping down what is pretty
To show what is real, honest as bone

And I never knew before that there was such grace
In emptying like this
In hollowing out like this
Becoming paper lantern like this –

Let me burn like the wick of me is sage brush
And will never run out
Let me burn so bright that my demons
Turn shadow puppet
On the outside of my skin

Let the smoke speak the things
I was never brave enough to say out loud
But here, let me find that there is nothing
Salt water cannot cure,
Preserving for future but drawing the poison out
Like this;

Here, let me find answers to the questions
I could only ask in salt
Let the ocean show me another word for *mercy*
Let me find a forgiveness that tastes
Like sage and saltwater and ash,

But here, now, before the endless sea,
I am a burning river

And the waves are leading me home.

50.719950, -2.800951

Letters to the wolf

i.

I was the first to call you the Old Wolf.
You turned country lanes to fairytale wilderness,
taught me to jump fences and duck
inconvenient 'keep out' signs.
Every track held a story.
Every map an adventure.
You made magic feel real,
and I have searched for the ghost of it
ever since you left.

ii.

When I was eight years old,
you brought home a rabbit
and taught me to skin it.
You always said I was too soft,
that I needed to toughen up.
That day I learned what happens
to soft things in this house.

iii.

You used to call me little bird.
I was the quieter of your daughters,
but each year I understood
when the swallows began to fly south.
September remains the month
I am most at peace with your memory.

Lessons from barn swallows

The summer wind brought me in and I came to rest
in the harbour where he found me;
Wind-circler, carrying horizons in my wing bars;
he looked at me like I was a picture book
from a library he never knew existed,
and me, weather-worn and storm-weary,
I stayed a while in his shelter
gave him sunsets and stories,
every brightly coloured thing I could
frame into words,
and he listened wide eyed and wondering,
read my travel scars like ley lines;
told me to my face we would be a disaster
and loved me anyway;
learned that my kin meant safe return and so,
he offered me anchor,
wore my smile like a lucky tattoo
and hoped to be my north star

And how could I not ask the wind
if there was a match for such courage?
When to fly like this is to know the pull of the blue
where all is vivid and dangerous and alive
in ways that he, who has never left shore
cannot comprehend,
and yet he let me fly,
if only to count on my returning.
Took to watching summer skies for me
and leaving the window open

until he saw the airborne skeins drawn south,
until the air turned cold
until he began resenting the north wind
and came to curse what it is
to love a wild bird with stories but no land.

And so the man I have no business loving
but do anyway
now takes to avoiding the ocean and
closing his window to keep out the wind
and the thought of me,
redrawing lines that I had made blue and blurry,
a kaleidoscope of futures we knew
we could not have
but oh, the weight of these eyelash rainbows;
these stubborn summer storm electric charges.
Who knew that a warm breeze could feel
so much like lead ballast; like deep winter,
when once, we were August.

So, I circle
knowing that he will never see
the wild beauty beyond the shoreline.
Learn to swallow envy for those
he will one day call home,
because what was this if not impossible?

Perhaps one day,
he will look up with his new lover
and a summer sky will again just be
a summer sky –
Not a missed chance.

A long ago love song.
And maybe, I will be there,
still circling the air currents,
returning to a place I once called safe haven
and telling the wind our story.

I'm not sure I know how not to.

The real marvel here

It takes 34 muscles for the human hand to form a fist.

It takes more than 50 muscles for a handshake.

From this I am choosing to learn
that the true test of a hero is to extend an olive branch
instead of grasping a sword.

The comic books I read never taught me these numbers
And I am still learning to be better at maths.

Honesty at 88mph

I think I just had the most honest conversation of my life,
travelling up the M40 after a perfect summer's day.

This is how I remember it –

We are driving through a patchwork of cloud and our hands are
draped easy over the other, singing along to Boyce Avenue covers
of pop songs I should know better than to know the words to.
The thing about being in a car with someone is that though the
engine and the road make you turn up the radio to drown out the
noise, the metal and glass catches the sound of your heartbeats
until they are a part of the bassline – spark ignite strike –
And this is a moment out of time which they are only reminding
us must come to an end.

This morning we were by the sea, and the smell of saltwater and
warm stone has stuck to your clothes like it knows I want to
remember. We have always been too honest, but I don't have the
heart to say that it will be years before I can walk the shoreline
without thinking about you, and everything we didn't name in the
silences between our fingertips, and the things that we didn't do
in the breath's space between us when the wind stopped and the
barley stood still and even the gulls went quiet –

But this is a moment out of time. We are driving over the speed
limit, travelling towards a place where there is both a yesterday
and a tomorrow, and the mechanism of the thing we still have not
named is spinning almost as fast as my head every time I defy the
laws of physics and choose not to kiss you; but in the right now

we are sat together in the drop forge echoes of everything that *could be,*

And isn't that the crux of it? How we have found ourselves here, on a sun drenched motorway under a mackerel sky holding onto each other like we're holding on to maybe, push-pull tiding ourselves through all the waves of *what if* –

And really, what if? What if we forgave ourselves the honesty and static humming between the sentences and the damned imper-manence of it all? What if we named it? Wrote it in the sand and let the tide swallow it, if only for a moment? What if we just stayed here – a second, an hour, longer?

But this is a moment out of time and we have written ourselves in the sand of an hourglass we have tilted until the grains move wrong, and we have dropped all pretences and

The thing about being in a car with you is that every minute is another message in a bottle thrown to the currents wishing that maybe if we just move fast enough we can go back,

And right here in this car, speeding up a motorway and simultane-ously suspended in time until even the sun stands still, I hand you a feather to weigh my heart against; knowing you've held both long enough to judge but trusting you not to,

And the sun is flooding the wet concrete under the mackerel clouds and all laws of physics are, for right now, suspended,

And I tell you,

"You know, let's just keep driving fast. Just in case."

50.621163, -2.277161

Letters to the wolf

i.
Papa, I don't think I grew up the way you intended.
There is no manual for this.

ii.
I still carry your expectation in my pockets.
It measures time in achievements you would not be proud of.

The toll

A man told me a love story once in a bar in France.
He grinned over his wine and proudly
showed me his wedding band.

On a walking tour of Seville, I handed
the grief I wore like a coat to a girl from New Zealand
and watched her toss it into a fountain with a copper coin.
I still believe in sun and wishes.

On a crowded train from New Street,
a woman with blue hair and laugh lines gave me
the boy she once loved who died a soldier.

Above a beach in Cornwall I was given
a demon in a bottle by a man who wore his trauma
painted over with bad tattoos.

I once gave my worst transgression to a drunk student
sat on the pavement outside an ice cream shop
where the church bells rang over our heads.

In a hushed hostel dorm in Bournemouth,
a nurse gave me her third miscarriage
and the joy she found after the flood.

I once spoke my rapist's name
in a coffee shop full of poets in Birmingham
and only the walls flinched.

This is what we give to strangers
in places where nobody knows our names.

So many pieces of lives exchanged.
So many stories not my own that will not sit still
or turn into poems in my hands.

These are the things I carry,
and I do not know what to do with them.

The girl with all the gifts

The story says that I was a punishment. A curse moulded out of clay and set loose like buckshot. That I brought curiosity and terror followed in my wake; but hear me now.

I was the all-giver. I walked among men clothed in stolen flame and I carried a jar filled with hope. The story now says that I brought sin and trouble, and that hope was the only thing that was left behind, but the story is wrong.

Hope was the biggest gift I could bring you.

Like you, hope is an underdog.

It is bruised, and bloody and undignified. It is standing up again after the tenth knockout just to get back in the ring.

Hope already knows it can't win. Winning was never the point.

Hope climbed out of ice and darkness with frostbitten hands and a broken leg.

It entered a marathon it was barred from.

It didn't give up its seat on the bus.

It followed a fence for nine weeks to find its way home.

It cut off its own arm with a pocketknife.

Hope threw the first stone and it lay down its arms.

Don't tell me this is weakness. This is Steve Rogers before the symbols. This is holding onto tomorrow with torn off fingernails and shredded palms.

It is testifying in court.

It is standing escort outside the clinic.

It is holding hands in the street.

It is setting afloat on the ocean in a rubber dinghy.

The story says that I brought trouble, and it is right. I carried no tools of empire and conquest down the mountain.

I brought fire. I brought change. I brought with me the power to bring them down.

Some will tell you that hope is not a course of action.

But we are still here. We can do this all day.

No jar could ever contain that.

About what the neighbours saw

or didn't see –
or how we imagine they didn't –
how the rain was warm and
settled over this city like a blanket
how the sound of everything was
muted and wet and
the grass was softer than sin
how we didn't even make it to the door
how the storm clung to our skin for days
how even the sodium lamps
turned their faces away
how we didn't care what God witnessed
how next door's kitchen light came on
and could not reach us
how every lightning flash was a siren
how nobody thought to call emergency
how we were the only thing burning
in a city soaked with rain.

And all at once

The finger posts end, and I am spat into the streets of a nowhere town the decade forgot.

It is bank holiday Sunday and the streets heave, filled with soft pale bodies that smell of sunblock and ice cream, accents that do not belong here jarring in alleyways.

Behind me somewhere are the lonely miles of gorse and grass-choked trails that led me here, only a turn or two ago but evaporating before I can grasp the details. It feels more dream, less memory; odd moments sticking but the order jumbled.

Gone is the ever-present rush of water, drowned under car stereos and wine-soaked bravado. Everyone is shouting at once and my head is a hollow drum the noise inhabits.

From a run-down arcade, a jumble of tinny sounding game jingles spill onto the pavement where men in scuffed trainers prop open the door to smoke. They eye me for a second; frown; take another drag on their cigarettes.

I make my way through the clutter dodging plastic buckets and spades, caught in the in-between, when a Brummie drawl cuts through the din and I am momentarily displaced, realities forked.

In one, I am passing through the Bullring on my way home. I am tired from a day at work, and upset with my boss. I am concrete here. A weary kind of permanent.

In the other, there is nowhere I am going back to. I am a tumble-weed traveller passing through, noted more as negative space than nuisance.

My thoughts taste too loud.

There, the other me shouts too much. She is full and the fullness spills out, all belly laugh and tart contradiction.

Here, I am a hermit crab with no shell to crawl into.
I think I had one, once. Before. But now I am scraped down by the path; as much a part of it as it is of me. It feels like wildness.
Like simultaneously traversing and becoming.

In the other universe, the other me boils the kettle and uses cooking tongs to get the pasta down from a high shelf.
The man whose jumper she has borrowed will be home soon and a country album is playing with the volume turned up high.
There is realness in this. A steady grounding without demands.

In this, I know I am here by the rasp of my rucksack against the open welts on my back. The pain has faded into white noise, the kind I have to concentrate to notice again. Dust and grit cling to my legs, and there is no jumper to borrow. The pasta for dinner is a Tesco meal deal eaten alone by the harbour.

I do not remember the last time I had a conversation.
Or showered.

Around me, tourists argue and take selfies while the gulls eye their chips.

They do not see me leave.

Within moments the cacophony fades and I am present. Soft ground, cool breeze, raw back. Familiar and known. I nestle my tent beneath the boughs of a hedge and listen to the crows from the cocoon of my sleeping bag.

In the morning, there will be no trace left that I was here.

In the other place, that me curls onto the chest of the man whose jumper she still wears. There is something on the TV, but it is less there than she is. She falls asleep in the middle of the episode, and cannot imagine being anywhere else.

And not for the first time, I wonder which of us is real.

50.100802, -5.126018

Broadsands

Once, when I was twelve years old, I told you I did not want to run.
Right there our twin wills collided;
The first small rebellion. The first quiet break.

You looked me in the eyes and told me you do not hang around
with quitters
before you left me standing on the edge of the rugby pitches
and walked away to carry on alone.

Right then, I learned two fundamental things.
First, I had to find a new way to make you love me.
And second, choosing my own way will never make you proud.

It has been ten years since you reversed the lesson and gave up
while I left you dying in a hospital bed and walked away to carry
on alone,
the weight of your disappointment one I had long grown used to
bearing.

Regardless of this, I still cannot find it in me to quit running.
Even when I know you would have.
Even when I know that I should.

They made this place a verb

They rebuilt this city from smoking rubble and stubbornness.

I refrain from asking what happened in the gracious old house
by the station.
Still empty, lilacs and briars creeping through empty socket
windows,
an ugly kind of invisible beside the nice flats and hip conversions
down the street.
No twentysomethings here drinking cheap wine, no children
running wild on the lawn.

There is an unsigned building on this street where they never
filled in the bullet holes in the basement.
It's probably the most honest thing in this part of town.

Can buildings be haunted by the things their walls have witnessed?
Can I?

Five years later, and they have painted the stonework yellow.

A young family has moved into the roof apartment.
They like the Beatles – *Sergeant Pepper* floating down on summer
breeze.
The woman on the first floor has planted red begonias in a box on
her balcony.
I wonder if the walls remember or if their memories, too, have
been painted over.

The ghosts are so loud here.

Like the concrete never really stopped smoking, or
like the fear never got jetwashed out of the floor boards, or
like any station name can end a story, or
like border guards still make me nervous, or
like the river doesn't know where the bones in its bed came from,
or
like the boatman is still waiting on downpayment, or
like adrenaline comes free with the air, or
like all this will finally wash away someday,

Like I am here waiting for rain in the street,
my soles vibrating with air raid sirens
and names.

51.029833, 13.703441

An amateur sermon on blacksmithing

after Jess May Davies

When he comments on my temper
says I have become a sword,
I tell him how they are made.
How you heat the metal until it shrieks, watch
as the glow turns it into something malleable.

Bend it to the shape of your hammer,
again
and again
let the anvil bring it out of the flames and closer
to what you saw in it once.

Strike the metal until you are sure the echoes
will follow it into whatever dreams
unmade things have.

When you think it is beginning to look finished,
put it back into the fire.
This is where the magic starts.

They call this the Devil's Heart;
where the heat is fiercest and all the weak
parts of the steel melt away to a single ember
all break and burn and rage

Stoke the flames until they roar destruction
inside your forge.
Make Hell jealous.

When, at last, the blade is red and sleek and furious,
plunge it into the trough.
Ensure the water is cold enough to harden the steel's heart,
hold your breath as it hisses.
Stand well back from the steam that billows in protest.

When he asks me why choose a thing of such violence
I tell him that this is not really a metaphor.
That I can cut the hand that wields me as easily as not.
That I was made to protect
but do the opposite more often than I don't,

And this is not always a contradiction
but the forge I was made in.

Have you ever noticed how a blade is only named
after the tempering?
As if its survival is the defining fact of it.
As if the steel is no longer what was done
but don't we always remember the name of the blacksmith
who made it?
Note his stamp upon the tang?

And should I, then, give credit
to my own crucibles?
To Daniel,
the lion's den I learned to sleep in?
Or Patrick,
who made me shed my own skin
to withstand the purge of him?
Survival isn't always courageous.

It's not always even earned.
Sometimes, it is only the anvil
and passive making of a thing
from the fire and hammer blow.

And I think he forgets that
there are only edges here.
Sees only how I balance;
The very least dangerous parts of me
held,

A perfect fit inside his hand.

Lies I have told

The bus was late.
Of course I did my homework,
       it's on my desk at home.
My phone had no signal.
It's only a little mountain,
       you'd hardly call it a hike at all.
I would *never* forget our anniversary.
I absolutely understand what you are saying.
No, doesn't hurt at all.
I'm doing great, thanks.
Gefilte fish is the best thing ever!
Of course this is what I want.
I don't understand what you are saying.
I love you.
Nah, they'd never kill Ned Stark off,
       he's like the hero of the whole show.
I fell.
It's ok, I had a big breakfast.
It's ok, I had a big lunch.
No, I don't want to talk about it.
What, me?
       Of course I didn't cry when Dumbledore died.
He loves me.
It was an accident.
I'm sorry.
I wish I never met you.

Letter to The Golden Gate Bridge

If I must go first, do not bury me in black and sing hymns.

Instead, turn my body into a salvage site.
Take me apart like a rusted ship and sort the remains for pieces
you can make new.

Turn my ribs into a doorframe,
Make it big enough to hold everyone I love inside it. They've had
practice, there's room to spare.

Return the flock of birds in my chest to my husband's laughter
It's where they were most at home anyway

Open my arms into a bedframe to hold his sleep safe.
Some things are too sacred to change.

Make my hands into a herb garden so they can be nothing but
gentle.
Tell my knuckles it's ok to unclench; plant flowers where they
resist the softening.

Melt the barbed wire in my throat to make a penny whistle.
The music will take time, but you will hear it when the razors
finally un-scar.

Weave my hair into a talisman to guard your daughter's dreams
Tell her bedtime stories about girls who became dragons so she
learns not to fear the dark;

When you pull the grenades from my ribs, use them as fireworks
so she never wants for a night lamp
Turn my ugly into a beacon to guide her where you can't reach.

Decant my grin into a sea bottle and keep it in the kitchen,
Make sure you season generously and that the food makes you
laugh into your wine –
Make it a good bottle.
Turn every giggle into a special occasion.

Hang my voice among the chimes on the porch to sing you better
days coming when the breeze is still
Because better days are coming, I promise.

I know it looks dark now sometimes, but
The birds know.

When you doubt, sit in my husband's kitchen and share a drink.
Tell stories.
Laugh like I can still hear you.

Outside, the birds will flock and settle on telephone wires,
the wind alive with feathers and song.

20 postcards

Dear Scotland,
I'm not big on writing home, but I
Sure seem to write to you a lot.

Dear Devon,
It's not that I don't love you.
I think we outgrew each other.

Dear Germany,
You taught me what love feels like.

Dear Oxford,
Just remember, it's Georgian rather than old, ok?

Dear Spain,
It's complicated.

Dear Scotland,
I wrote poems about you.

Dear Birmingham,
It's not you, it's me.

Dear Paignton,
When did you get old?
I didn't notice the shine wearing off until
I'd already gone.

Dear Seville,
Thank you for redemption.

Dear Manchester,
I don't know.
I'm sure we'll work it out some day.

Dear Israel,
You're in my blood
But I hardly remember you.

Dear Canada,
Say hi to the Northern Lights for me.

Dear Oxford,
You were an ill-fitting coat,
I can't help but admire your style.

Dear Birmingham,
I think it's the soot.
And the traffic hum.

Dear Tours,
It was a wonderful affair.

Dear Schwarzwald,
I think your stories still whisper to me.

Dear Aragon,
We never stood a chance.

Dear mountains,
Your shoulders feel like my father's.

Dear Scotland,
Let's share a dram some time.
See if we can work this thing out.

Dear Scotland,
Tell me some stories.
There are letters home I have still to write.

56.618853, -4.800784

Letters to the wolf

i.

I cannot remember the smell of your hugs
without disinfectant and hospital sheets burning my nose.
There is no manual for this.

ii.

I stared down a feral dog yesterday
and it is the closest I have been
to speaking to you in years.

When the wave breaks

There are things I remember with the vividness of lost dreams the
moment after waking up.

When I write about him, it is the dreams which come back to me
first, wash up flotsam of things I have held fish hooked on my
tongue –
but I remember it all. I think.

Sand, black at first glance but splintering rainbow in sunlight
crystal as the salt of oceans dreamed –

I was dreaming of oceans.

The taste of salt and blood and other things in the blurred lines
between dreaming and awake;
when they warned me about this, it was always so clear – *no* always
meant stop.
But this is something that happened to strangers who didn't avoid
dark alleyways and I
was always careful of streetlights
I knew *no* meant something
was powerful
was violent and ugly and so
I held it like a razor between my teeth, swallowed it whole –
no was too big, too much like a broken bottle promise,
hands I did not know in that moment making Braille of my
creeping skin and
I do not know where the lines became clear –

When I googled 'was it rape?' for the sixth time last night, it tasted
of salt.
There are fingerprints like bruises I never show in public, bruises
that were never bruises because of a *no*
I cannot remember and cannot prove happened

I thought I said *no*.

To the hand at once his and a stranger's,
breath on my neck tasting of salt and other and

I was dreaming of oceans.

Thought I was still dreaming of oceans,
thought it was all a strange turn in a dream within a dream and I
cannot remember but
I thought I said *no*.

There is no jury that will believe me when I say
I did not want this;
that a ring and a precedent meant anything other than yes;
a story lit green with gas lights the only time I have dared
speak my account to a friend
But I have never said a yes that was so much like salt water, like
driftwood tongue caught on teeth, like –

When I asked him what happened, he told me
that if I had only put out more, he might have been able to control
himself.
But it wasn't what it sounds like. After all, it had been fun, right?

It has taken me two years to lance the no from that night,
and I still cannot bring myself to call it

a trespass, a ransacked house
that feels like the aftermath of an unwanted guest, see
how I still have not called it by name?
Said no.

I will not call myself victim.

Nobody prepares you to be the casualty who walks away from the
crash and
claims fault for the shattering;

I fell into the bed of the first
man to treat my yes like it meant something, and it was not re-
venge.
I said yes and it was the first time I saw my body as anything other
than a crime scene.

There are fingertip bruises on parts of me that have since only
ever been
handled with care,
and I still cannot bring myself to name it –

ugly

tasting of oceans I thought I had dreamed but left tracks that
itched when I woke,
cracked frames from a dream blurred
by guilt and doubt and every name I could call it
other than one;

It has taken me two years to return to the ocean

and wake up.

Questionable business

You left me with
a fistful of poems
and a leather jacket;
I'd call it a good deal
but I don't make bargains
at crossroads anymore.

Tasseography

I offer her a cup of tea.
There are no names for the river under this bridge, so I make tea, stir in milk and sugar the way she always liked, let the pot sit between us filled with six months of conversations we haven't had. I tell her I'm sorry.

Tea is what we offer when there is nothing left for us to say, when there is so much water that we must drink it or drown in all the things left unspoken, so we fill the kettle.
There is a ritual to it, you know. To preparing the leaves – I always use loose leaves if I can get them – heating the pot and swirling the heat up the sides so that your liquor doesn't taste like an old broom. There is a knack in letting the kettle thrumble to exactly the right pitch to turn off the heat, well before it over-boils and starts to taste off.
When you fill the pot, you hit the sides first, not the leaves or you might cook them, and let the water turn that ambery shade some-where between good bourbon and beech leaves in October.

It reminds us of the good times, hot mugs cradled in blue fingers after autumn walks, sat in my horrible old flat with the broken heating and the dodgy fire alarm.
She sips, eyes closed on memory, swirls the liquid round her mug.

We once hopscotched cultures and languages, exchanging recipes over pots of cheap PG Tips.
When the summer ripened I iced jugs of peppermint and hibis-cus, and when disaster struck we sat on the grass and sipped and sunburned, and the rain felt like an age of drought away.

She swirled the liquid then, and the words came slowly, like steam. They come slower now.

She jokes about a trip we once planned.
My smile is more memory than reflex, but it comes. I tell her there's always next year.
When there is nothing else left to offer, tea is a reassuring blanket that wraps us in better yesterdays.
We both know there will probably not be a next year, but the tea is warm and we sip, swirl the mugs, try to drink the water lapping at the bridge.

I check the dregs, and there is maybe half a cup's peace left in the bottom before we hit stone.
I want to break the silence, want to ask her all the questions that sit in the bilge at the bottom of the pot like *Where were you? Where did you go?*

There are things in that water that are better left drowned, that do not belong in this room but the questions taste metal and heavy on my tongue.
She has not drunk the remainder of her tea, so I mention this instead.
'I don't take sugar any more,' she says, a small shrug under the jumper.

I don't say anything, just pour away the mug, make her a fresh one, no sugar this time.
When you read the dregs of a cup, there is a ritual to it – handle first, clockwise round the rim and spiralling down; you can read a person's soul in the pattern of the tealeaves left from a well enjoyed brew.

I do not know what the rule is for a cup not drunk, but nothing says *I no longer know you* quite like not knowing how someone takes their tea.

There is Assam in the pot today. It is the first tea we drank together, and this is apt.
We drank it rich with spice and good hope, and the name itself speaks.
It means *unequalled.*
Or, *unequal.*
I do not know which applies in these circumstances, but they both describe what we were, what we have been.
The leaves hold no answers this time, and there is so much water under this bridge.

I do not know how to stem this river, and the rains have come and gone unnoticed.
There are things we have not said, things we should have said, but the words lie drowned in the dark at the bottom of the brew.
How do you drink this much water and not choke?

The pot says nothing on the matter and the dregs have gone bitter, so I follow the old ritual.
Put the kettle on.
Stir in milk but no sugar, the way she likes now, let it sit between us on the table.
I tell her I am sorry.
Swirl the amber, take a sip,
and feel the flood waters rise.

An inventory

lost:

- In a bathroom stall at Leicester services
- Three seconds before the leap
- In the big interview you waited a month for
- On the floor of your ex's bedroom, drunk

found:

- Between heartbeats, immediately after the fall
- On the predawn walk home from across town
- Outside the Fighting Cocks, smoking a cigarette
- Folded in a pocket of the dress he hated

Letters to the wolf

i.

September still brings the south yearning.
The man I love does not understand this
but I pretend you would like him anyway.

ii.

What you taught me about defence did not protect me.
I do not blame you for this.
Soft things do not survive in this house.

iii.

I have learned the hard way
that I am stronger than a skinning knife.

50.424374, -3.566900

Reunion

Hello –
You're here.
And I have no idea how to talk to you.

Hi –
I've been choosing these words for years
In case they're the last ones we'll ever share.

How have you been?
There are lies I practiced in the mirror
until I almost believed them myself.

Yes I've been well –
I haven't stopped watching the moon
since you vanished.

Thank you;
Sometimes I wonder if
I imagined you.

I've been busy, you know–
I can map every freckle the sun has
put on your face since the last time
I kissed you.

What are you up to these days?
Where do you go to that is off the map
of us you once drew on my palm?

Are you happy?
Did it hurt when you erased me?

How's your family?
I will never be able to un-know
the gentle of you.

I'm glad you're doing well.
There are letters I am afraid to write you
but you appear in so many poems
you've become an accent my mouth cannot un-learn.

Hello –
I have said good-bye to you so many times
I no longer trust the moon.
And you're here.

On loving an alpinist

for Emilie Forsberg and Sanni McCandless

He will enter your life like a summer hailstorm.
No warning.

When you meet him, the sun will stop.
It will be somewhere innocuous –
Across the office breakroom; on the train platform; out for
coffee on Sunday...
But you will know instantly.

Or else –
He will blow through like winter on an evening like any other.
You will be at dinner with friends and forget
everything that was served to eat.
He will carry sunsets and glaciers, and you
will fall asleep wondering which river he was drawing
in the drop of wine spilled from his glass.

His hands will be rope burned and oil-stained.
You will rarely see him in anything but boots and fatigues
but you will look at him each time like he is waiting by a
marble staircase
you are descending in spun glass slippers.

He will make you believe in magic,
because how else to explain all this wonder?

There will be no alpenglow like his smile
watching meadow sunrises.

You prefer your coffee the way he drinks it
before kissing you awake on his way out.

When he leaves,
you will dream coffee steam and kitchen humming for days.

He will not call.
There is no signal in the wild,
and his heart is the wildest of places –

Your messages will come back piecemeal:
Unable to deliver. Recipient could not be reached.

But you knew this was coming.

The birds make vapour trails south
while he is away.

You bake bulk of the white loaves he loves for breakfast
and eat none of them.
You measure the time he is gone
in stale bread.

He taught you to love the winter, but now
you cannot stand the smell of snow-dusted firs
because it will be the smell of the phone call.

You debate with yourself whether to stand vigil by the door
or rip the landline out of the damn wall.

You never knew days so short
could pass so slowly.

You curse the falling leaves
for the colours he showed you in them.

His footsteps are a gunshot silence beside you
on the trail you love to walk together.

You begin watching the birds for smoke signals.

And then one night, he will come home.
Like a snap thaw.
No warning.

You will want to yell,
to curse
you will want to kiss him
until the grey hairs fade and
the holes wear back into the kitchen tiles;

His eyes will stop you.
His hands will be the northern lights you waited
the whole winter to see.

And when he returns to you,
he will ask you again to see the high summits
the beauty he has always walked alone

You will only ever be able to answer,
"Oh but love, I have. I have."

When I say I love you, know this

You were never mine
but God damn if I wouldn't have
laid my very bones as a bridge
to ease your way.

And I think it is kinder like this.

Where I cannot hold you
to a rusted claim
but instead am the smoothest road;
someone for you to pass through
on your way someplace else
where you will speak of a long journey
and sleep peaceful

Dreaming you are afloat in the arms of an ocean.

Nereid

[Ephesians 4:32]
Get rid of all bitterness, rage and anger,
brawling and slander,
along with every form of malice.
Be kind and compassionate to one another,
forgive.

May the waves wash this clean.

It is not in me to stay quiet.
Let me sharpen my teeth,
let my tongue grow forked
my scalp wreath with snakes,
let this body become toxic.

Bring me holy water.
Give me wine-bloodied lips.
Give me a bed of thorns
and let me enjoy it.

I no longer dream of oceans.

Instead, let my dreams be hurricane.
Let the boats wreck
let the water become graveyard,
let it swallow all comers,
and may the waves wash this clean.

There is no softness left in me.
I no longer dream of oceans.

Fire and steel can't touch me now.
I have poisoned the ink well I draw from.
I have laid snares in every doorway.
I have boarded every window.

Let all the mirrors shatter.
Let the cracks name the thing that lives
where he trespassed
let all the lightbulbs blow out
let me hear you say forgiveness.

There is no softness left here.
All I have to offer is my rage.

And may the waves wash this clean.

Letters to the wolf

i.

Part of me is glad you will never read my poems.
Another wants to scream them at the boatman until
he tells you I did something worthwhile when you weren't looking.
There is no manual for this.

Hearth magic

Some things, you did not need to ask.

I, melted ricepaper under rain.

You, a haven.

The answer came unspoken and began here –

Rosemary, for clarity.

Marjoram, for finding joy again.

Garlic, to draw the poison.

Lemon, for the bright clean of someday.

Your kitchen became alchemy
and I have never felt so safe.

52.459045, -1.906445

The application form asks about my ethnic background

Ask my mother where she is from, and she will not tell you. She tucks her accent under berets and pearl strings, takes offence at anyone who questions her Britishness.
If you insist she is foreign, she will take it as a compliment when you assume she is French.

My mother is a stubborn survivor, a tree who uprooted herself and resettled twice in soil more to her liking, who gifted me with two tongues and a chameleon name.

My mother taught me to hold my language like a fake passport, made sure that I could blend in anywhere; slowly weaned me off the milk-tongue she gave me as a child, and showed me how to charm myself invisible.

My mother taught me to put on identities like I would put on outfits. Assimilation is the biggest survival tool she knows.
From her I learned to wear each one differently like a tailor made piece as occasion demands, and never let the style wear me.
It doesn't do to carry a coat that you cannot then shrug off when needed.

I watched her take her fourth language, break it to heel, make it sit up straight and teach it back to native speakers like she was born to it.

My mother taught me how to wear accents like make up.
How to swipe on red lipstick and a university cadence when you
mean business.
How doors always open if everyone believes you have a key.
How an imposter is always outed by their shoes, or their hands.
How to never say that these are all Russian proverbs.

My mother taught me to use my language like a switch blade.
Like a lock pick.
Like my mouth will spill *mazel-tov* at a promotion, *spasibo* in
thanks and declare *que j'en ai ras le bol* with all this
Verschlimmbessern with equal comfort –
and still know to take lemon with an Earl Grey tea.
But I am learning to wield my voice like a hatchet: with two good
hands and no apologies.

I wish sometimes she had named me more boldly.
Wish I carried a name that was unapologetic in its roots, that de-
manded thought before its use.

But when I tell my mother that I feel like I could be from anywhere, this is her gift to me.
When I tick the forms to say "White, British" and nobody looks
twice at my answer,
this is her biggest success.

So I have rooted myself with words and built myself a home in
the country I wrote here.
I do not tell her the stories and voices I am choosing to share.

I check the form again.

There is no box to tick for "I am from nowhere and everywhere, all at once. Just ask my mother."

I tick "White, British". Mentally add, *today.*

Letters to the wolf

i.
Why do you never answer my letters?

Shrapnel stitches

I dreamed of you again tonight and woke in a sweat for all the
wrong reasons.
The clock tells me it's 3am but where you are it's still daylight
I guess that's why I'm awake.
It has been 3 years, 6 months and 22 days since I last saw your
face but I remember you perfectly.
I remember your smell, still look twice when someone passes me
in the street with your stride
I still know the name of every star that shone through the cloud
and the light pollution on the night you showed them to me
I still know you.
You were the first.

You spoke my name like a promise; promised me dreams and
whispered secrets,
Found my edges and saw a puzzle you could study for a lifetime
and never get bored of looking.
You saw every scar I had and did not recoil.
Kissed them and called them sacred; turned my skin into a
treasure map and you the only one to break the code.
You took the weapons out of my hands and you became a blade I
used on myself.
Sometimes I'm sure a shard of you is still lodged in me
somewhere –
Hiding under my skin like shrapnel.
I heal clean but it aches when it's cold and I forget that I'm too
young to have weather bones.

You took the compass I held upside down, became my lodestone
Now I don't know how to navigate without the wall at my back
And I miss the certainty that comes with having only one possible
option
Miss waiting for the order to fire
Miss the spark in the barrel
Miss the blink
Miss the strike
I miss you.

> *Stop thinking.*
> *Switch sides.*
> *Just listen to the clock and sleep.*

Tick.

You have artist's hands.
Your fingers tune the strings of your bass like you're
weaving our stories in sound.

Tick.

You're stroking the neck of the bottle.
You are three drinks too far and I am three feet too close.

Tick.

Cold clear skies speak frost but the sun is warm on my back.
I keep that picture in a frame because I have never smiled
that way since.

Tick.

Your eyes have gone black.
But at least now we match.

Tick.

We're eating strawberries on the grass and you've made me
laugh so hard my ribs ache with it.

Tick.

You have artist's hands.

Tick.

You stroke the neck of the bottle.

Tick.

My neck is not glass.

Tick.

Head meets wall.

Tick.

The wall is my compass.

Stop.

Black.

Stop.

Black.

Stop.

Black.

Stop

Bright
on
black.

You showed me the stars.
And you could name every one.
And your smile is sunlight.

Tick.

You have artist's hands,
And I am your canvas

Tick.

I don't miss the excuses – scarves in the lecture halls, long sleeves
in summer.

Don't miss thinking fast for reasons to give my mother for my quiet
–
"Got the bruises at training"
"Got the bruises out hiking"
"Got bruised moving furniture"
"Caught in a commuter train"
"Slipped the curb"
"Bruises, what bruises?"
"It's nothing"
"I fell"
"It's nothing."
You were the first.

You are the reason nobody ever heard my poetry, too scared to
stand up and speak.
Afraid all they would see is just another cliché.
Another weakness.
You promised you would always be with me, now I can't look in the
mirror, expecting to see you over my shoulder.
The words come out wearing my voice and still all I can hear is you.
Strip my skin, you'll find yours under it.

Now for every nightmare when I wake, heart pounding, flinching at
shadows
there are too many nights when I dream of you
and regret waking to find you're not there.
Sometimes I can't help it – brush the thread in my mind that has
always been yours just to know you're still with me somehow.

Maybe it's physics.
Magnet drawn to iron, you are still a blade and I still have a
fascination with sharp edges.

Maybe it's because the marks have faded, and X no longer marks the spot,
but some days the shrapnel moves – and too often the sensation is pleasant.

Maybe one day I'll wake and not wish you were here.
Maybe that's the day I'll finally stop loving you the way I could never love myself.
But I wonder if I will ever stop writing poems about you
and I don't know if I want to.

The clock tells me it's 3.05am.
Where you are it's still daylight; nothing for it but to wait.
Lie quiet until you sleep peaceful and your dreams will graze the edges of mine.
It's the closest I get now to being near you.

It's ok, I'll be quiet I promise.
I won't move.
Won't speak.
I won't even dare to pray.

47.982900, 7.849616

We once walked a beach together

And before he lost me I said,
'Remember this always –
the way the tide will.'

After the fire

After Cam

Do you remember
standing together in a burning house pretending
not to see the flames while the roof crashed round our ears.

We don't talk about what we lost in the fire,
don't talk about the how or the why
or the scraps of a dream we refused to wake up from.

Now, my hands smell like your cigarettes and
you find strands of my hair in your coat
long after the summer's gone.
We wander familiar tracks, follow our feet back to ruins

Keep company with ghosts to revisit foundations we built,
now just dust lines in the grass we let grow over them
but where I still hear your laugh echo between walls that no
        longer stand
and skeleton lintels mourn the bricks we laid one by one.

We sit amongst the weeds that used to be a kitchen,
turn the patch of cloud above into a skylight,
don't talk about the firefighters,
the friends running buckets yelling to get out;

I don't know who carried the oil and who the matches
but we built this together then burned it down
and I still carry kindling in the jeans pockets
you used to slip your hand in when we walked.

We've been dreaming about the blaze for months,
wake every time clinging on to the memory of a home,
not talking about the wreckage we made

We've never felt more alive than right there,
so we say nothing and hold on to the smell of the ash,
ignore the sun and the sirens and blink away the aftershocks.

Peatbog magic

Today I ran to the water's edge;
followed my feet and the trail of a memory too old to be my own,
stranded here where marsh mist curls round my ankles,
a welcome to my steps.

I am sat on the bank of a river without a name, little more than
a blackwater trickle, where the air hums retreating summer and
bent-backed trees lean in to watch the clouds reflected.
People came here once to talk to their gods,
but I come here to talk to you.

You have never been here, the water whispers, peatbog promises of
secrets kept in the still. *Give me your troubles*, it says to me.
I will remember.

The procession of trees gathers where once there were priests,
wearing the mist as a shroud and reminds me I am on
hallowed ground.
What they left here was never meant to survive, black water
and rowan the only remaining gatekeepers.

Deep in this water there are treasures, gold and silver wrought and
then ruined, sacrificed to gods who knew that some things have to
be broken to be beautiful –
we were broken enough to be beautiful.
The gods have no use for things which could still live among us
and we have inflicted such damage on these memories that they
have become holy.

Everything that came here before me met a violent end,
and we are no different; but there is a comfort in knowing that
this is where ruined is a byword for sacred, every blemish perfect.
We are safe here, where only the trees will speak memorial.

And so, I empty my pockets of the things I have held onto long
after I should, every one exquisite and familiar and broken
beyond all recognition,
this is how I know that they are mine.
The people who made this path would have understood.

Let it go, the water tells me.

So I roll the memories between my fingers, multicoloured pieces
of us worn smooth with time and the rub of my hips as I walk,
count them out like prayer beads.
Here, the taste of cheap bourbon and lip-bite that I sipped
in December to spit out in July,
the way I drank until the alcohol no longer tasted like an apology.
Here, the stars in November, the scorch of fireworks
and toffee-apple kisses under rain-damp trees;
Here, how I re-read every poem I have written looking for your
fingerprints in the ink,
How I set fire to all the photographs but one; put it in a cast-iron
box with your voice so the magic couldn't seep out, hoped the
smoke wouldn't reach you;
Here, how I put my fist through the wall until it spelled I miss you
in Morse code, blackwater promises made in the fog before day-
break and burned off in the sun,
The scars we traded and then kissed and rescarred again until
they were broken enough to be ours, god-touched.

Hold it all in my cupped hands with the bones of what was –

Give it to me, says the water.

And I do.

Letters to the wolf

i.

I think I saw you on my way home
through Selly Oak the other night,
and for a moment the street-lamps
were indistinguishable from trees.

I don't need Adrenaline

The moment before freefall,
a skydiver's heartrate reaches over 170 beats per minute.

Free divers can hold their breath
for 10 minutes or more under water.

The Kuuk Thaayore tribe in Australia has no words
for *left or right*, but knows the cardinal direction of every step.

And here, with you, only just out of reach

    I know my way home.
    The air in my lungs is sweet and tastes like April.
    The earth is warm and steady beneath my feet.

    Yes.

50.536555, -4.214238

Alternatives to the word *fiance*

After Rudy Francisco

Master of the remote. Wizard of white sauce.
Kitchen alchemist. The one who taught me to
make bread. Navigator of the OS map. Befriender
of cats which *do not belong to us*. The good bottle
of whisky. The patient tread on the stairs.
Windstorm tamer. Safe harbour. Mirrored downhill
grin. Bringer of the spare waterproof jacket.
Unlooked-for porchlight. True North, the one
direction I always know I can trust.

Kelvingrove

i.
Under a bluebird sky that does not know my name
I am untethered as dandelion seed.
Above, the dome reaches endless;
sun beat and cricket pavilion percussion
anchors against the beckoning fall upwards
tart sweetness of season's harvest the gentlest pull
back to a present where this no longer means
memories of us.

ii.
The city I came to for healing has forgotten its bones.
From here, glory and shadow lay twined
distant hum of traffic muting the bees investigating rebellious
flowers
which bloom defiant of urban sophistication.
I cannot help but wonder what you would have made of it –
this strange skyline, the crows haunting the river,
skyscrapers and churches rubbing shoulders,
racing to reach god first.
I wonder idly which you would have bet on.
I wonder if you would have bet on me.

iii.
This place was named for a man who made his fame
by putting a quantity on the unquantifiable.
Like you, he had a disdain for the fanciful,
sure he could apply science to anything his gaze fell upon.
Once, he tried to reinvent the compass,
make sailors put away their lodestones and legends
in favour of cold equations and fact.
Once, I threw out all of my stories and poems,
because you told me my emotions were ridiculous.
He should have known that there are some things
you cannot break to logic.
You should have known that I would not remain silent for long.
Some things, only faith can touch.
It is apt then, perhaps, that it is here in the shadow
of vain mathematics and failed conviction
that I finally stepped into the sun.

55.870325, -4.282147

Maybe a day later

You follow the rules of Leave No Trace
better than anyone I know.

Determined to prevent damage
there is nothing to show that you were here

But an indentation where you stood;
so many soft footprints on my mind.

A true story

In the founding moment of our family
a girl running late for work
sticks out her thumb on the edge of a highway.

She stands, a statue in stress
and the big American car she knew
would never slow down
screeches to a halt
a hundred yards down on the hard shoulder
and reverses back to her.

The door opens. They stare.
He doesn't know her language
and she has forgotten the small talk phrases
of his that she learned in school.
She hesitates.
He smiles.
And history is made.

She tells him the name of the bank
where she works as a cashier.
He nods, indicates shotgun
and the journey passes in silence
the magic kind you get right before it snows,
their brains lost in translation
scrambling for dictionaries and phrase books.

He tells her it's no trouble
she thanks him in broken English
and decides she loves his smile
big and toothy
like the big bad wolf decided to play
and she was invited in on the game.

They go their ways, she to work
he to the coffee house he has adopted
as his office in the next town.
He changes his route to work
watching the road for black hair and her thumb;
she watches the road for his car
cuts her morning commute finer each day.

He tracks her to the bank
invites her for coffee
(thanking his lucky stars the word is universal)
and their story begins.

Chapter one

Years pass by and with them
he teaches her his language
and she speaks to him in so much more
than just language.
He shows her the world.
She makes him a home.
They travel.
They fight.
They marvel at the world and
everything in it.

They get married in London,
away from everyone they both know.
Her best friend is at her wedding only
by sheer cosmic coincidence.
The chapters turn and give them daughters,
the man with the wolf smile
and the girl by the highway,
fair and dark, night and day.
I am his turtle dove
She is chickadee.
They weave their legends around them
in gold thread, so that the very walls
gleam with stories
in the apartment where they live.

Time is kind to them,
and they take their monikers seriously
the Old Wolf
the bird girls
and the girl by the highway
grown now into Mother Bear
proud and obstinate
exactly the way he loves her.

He tells them stories
She teaches them lessons
They hold back the world with myth.
And on the night when blue lights
tear the threads in the walls
and take away the man with the wolf in his smile
lopsided now but still toothy
insisting to my mother
to stop being daft, I'll be fine in a minute

Her
world
just
stops.

The silence lasts for months, or a lifetime.
Then slowly, they begin to tell the stories again
spinning the legend of the man with the silver beard
and the wolf smile.
The bird girls have grown fierce –
call it growing into the wolf
and they hold his name to them
like a talisman against the dark.

Some days, Mother Bear paces the apartment
where they wove their tales
and wonders at how a place so small
can feel so very, very big
when once it was fit to burst
with all the life
and laughter and stories inside it.

She keeps his clothes on the chair
where he laid them, military neat that last night
as if she were waiting for him
to come in one morning and put them back on
while she is out tending flowers
by the granite marker she made him.

Husband
Father
Champion.

Tomorrow, somewhere,
a girl by the highway will stick out her thumb
waiting for the big American car
to screech to a halt by the hard shoulder.
She will stand, an echoing memorial
waiting for destiny
to pull over, and smile.

31.889650, 34.836790

There is only one constant

On the riverbank. In the corridor. In the laugh
ache. In the small hours. On the station platform.
In the stomach churn on the way home. In the 4am
pillow howl. In the concert crowd. In the loss
wrench. In the found weight. In the heavy. In the
water. In the razorblade. In the unstained carpet. In
the gospel word of unworthy. In my transgression.
In the hospital ward. In the first black eye. In the
third black eye. On the motorway bridge exit sign.
In the city I left burning. In the home he built from
my mute bones. In the pneumonia I ran through. In
the torn muscle I ran through. In the uninvited
hands I did not say no to. In the burnout. In the
shattering. In the empty hollow. In the seawater. In
the mercy. In the plane cabin that brought me back.
In the sand the tide took. In the sunrise. In the one
more day. In the porchlight. On the station
platform. In the small hours. In the laugh ache. In
the corridor. On the riverbank.

You were there.

You were there.

You were there.

Letters to the wolf

i.

Peace found me when I least expected it.
I do not recall where I left the guilt behind.
Perhaps the boatman took it with the last letter I sent.

ii.

The magic never left me, it turned out.
I do not know if I spent those years
chasing you down or trying to escape you,
but now I am running beneath a sky the colour of hope,
and your shadow cannot reach me here.

Sunday

Let's dance, you and me.
Leave the straight lines and the rules in the parking lot
and dare the wind to play catch up.

We'll barrel our way down root-choked paths
and take corners too tight for our talent;
slog up climbs like we're chasing redemption on every hilltop

And swear we find hope along every single-track we follow
where unanswered prayers make voltage pylons of our bones
and our legs start to buzz with the pent up wire and static.

Let's fly into the wind until the rain makes our faces numb
and we will laugh and let the ice melt baptise the wrong out of
our pasts
write our penance in mud track and shale

We'll scrape ourselves raw and scoop ourselves out;
turn valleys into confessionals, thermos tea into communion wine
and make jack-o-lanterns of our haunted hearts to light our return.

You and I know that a house of healing
doesn't need four walls or a roof when you have your feet in
the cloud,
this thorn-scrape-peat-stain-hunt-grin cathedral of shadows
and light.

Come on let's stand, you and me, on the shoulders of giants,
leave behind pieces of questions beat out on hillsides
so far apart only God can read them without skipping a line

Recited out by stubborn feet and tempest wills
we'll follow the music over moor and fell, read answers in contours;
code-lines so far apart maybe God was the one who left them there

Let's dance to the rhythm and drum and the reckless reels
of a landscape that sings to us in a language unwritten
until maybe, at last, we can follow the wild song back.

Let's run.

ACKNOWLEDGEMENTS

This collection has been on a long journey on its way to the book you hold in your hands, and would not exist but for the magic of good people helping me, and it, on our way.

To the trail – thank you for the words, and for redemption.

To Hazel Sealeaf, for appearing always at the right time, and for making the introduction to Stuart when I didn't have the belief or courage to do so myself.

To Stuart Bartholomew at Verve – for taking a chance and giving me an opportunity beyond anything I dared hope for. Thanks will never be enough.

To the Birmingham poetry community, thank you for adopting me, for the encouragement, and for collectively helping to hone my words into something meaningful. To Jasmine Gardosi, Nafeesa Hamid, Casey Bailey, Leon Priestnal, and Sean Colletti, for the gentlest mentorship.

To Rick Sanders, for the slot at Whisky & Words that changed everything, and for the chances to shine beyond that.

To Sarah Molloy and Rhiannon May – for showing that great leadership can be both strong and soft. Thank you for always supporting my ambitions outside the office as much as the ones inside it. I'm proud to call you my bosses.

To Jess Davies and Tim Scotson for their friendship and skilful edits. Your ability to understand what I am trying to say before I do is extraordinary. Thank you for the final shaping touches that made some of my favourite poems in this collection what they are.

To Daisy Edwards for asking the right questions, and being steadfast when I got the answers wrong. I am so excited to see where that brilliant mind takes you next.

To Tom Crossland, for everything. Thank you for being the first person to introduce yourself by quoting one of my poems back to me, for the 5am mythology discussions, for the instruction in lost arts (drop forge would never have made it here without you), and for showing me God in 3 equations. Your friendship is one of the best things to have come out of a poetry night.

To my trail running family: Cajsa, Claire, Emma, Melanie, Claudia, Coren, and so many others – you were there when nobody else could be, and believed in me when I couldn't. *Sunday* is for you.

To Brian Sharp – thank you for staying up late to talk me down from the edge on my last night on the Coast Path, for reading the first draft of a poem I didn't dare show anyone else yet, and unwittingly giving me a line about jack-o-lanterns that I love to this day.

To Al Cameron, for the many adventures. The road is less lonely when you're with me.

Charlotte Levin, Jon Boissonade and John Weaver – I wouldn't have made it far without you.

To Claire Gaffney, for being the first person I talk to about anything writing related for the last twenty years. We've come a long way from Blagdon.

To Chris – my North. Thank you for showing me the way when I was lost in the dark. I am so glad you said yes.

To my mother, for using "when you're a published author" as a reasonable statement for as long as I can remember.

And last, to my father, the Old Wolf – for teaching me that in the end we are all stories, and to make it a good one. What I wouldn't give to tell you mine in person. I miss you.

ABOUT VERVE POETRY PRESS

Verve Poetry Festival is a new press focussing initially on meeting a local need in Birmingham - a need for the vibrant poetry scene here in Brum to find a way to present itself to the poetry world via publication. Co-founded by Stuart Bartholomew and Amerah Saleh, it is publishing poets from all corners of the city - poets that represent the city's varied and energetic qualities and will communicate its many poetic stories.

Added to this is a colourful pamphlet series featuring poets who have previously performed at our sister festival - and a poetry show series which captures the magic of longer poetry performance pieces by poets such as Polarbear and Matt Abbott.

Like the festival, we strive to think about poetry in inclusive ways and embrace the multiplicity of approaches towards this glorious art.

www.vervepoetrypress.com
@VervePoetryPres
mail@vervepoetrypress.com